UNLOCKED

UNLOCKED

Reading & Writing Prompts
for Practising Poets

by

Sue Butler & Helena Nelson

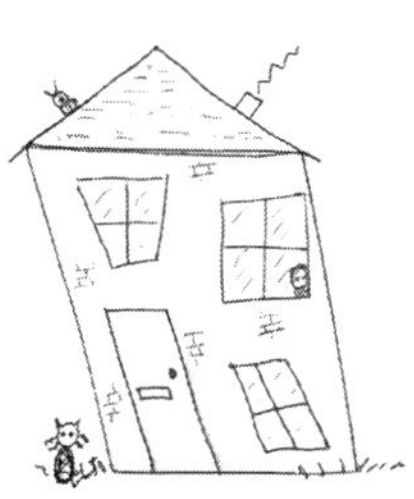

HAPPENSTANCE PRESS

ISBN: 978-1-910131-65-7

Warm thanks to the following authors, or their estates, who have given permission for poems to be included: Alan Buckley, Tom Duddy, Charlotte Gann, Fiona Moore, Stephen Payne, D. A. Prince. The copyright of the poems belongs to them.

BIOGRAPHICAL:

An Eric Gregory Award-winner, Sue Butler is the author of a number of *Learning to Improvise* (Rockingham), *Vanishing Trick* (Smith/Doorstop) and *Arson* (Happen*Stance)*. She has worked as a copywriter in Beijing and Malaysia. She is also poetry editor of *Writers' Forum.*

Helena Nelson is orginator/editor of Happen*Stance* Press, and author of *Starlight on Water* (Rialto 2003), *Plot and Counterplot* (Shoestring, 2010), *How (Not) to Get Your Poetry Published* (Happen*Stance* 2016), *Down With Poetry* (Happen*Stance* 2016), and *Branded* (Red Squirrel 2019).

First published in 2020 by Happen*Stance* Press
21 Hatton Green, Glenrothes KY7 4SD
https://happenstancepress.com

Printed and bound by Imprint Digital, Exeter
https://digital.imprint.co.uk

CONTENTS

Foreword

A TRUE POEM—the kind that lifts off the page and flies into the reader's heart—is a mysterious creature. But the skills and experience and practice that go into making such a thing are somewhat less mysterious.

A poet is a simply a writer who makes poems. And writers aren't born; they're made. Their training involves close reading, extensive immersion in language, and continuous practice. Most poets build a sizeable mountain of forgettable work before there's any chance of a poem that sings.

Even after decades of practice, each new poem is a unique challenge, and each poem that's read (not written) may teach something useful—a trick, a shape, a form; or even what *not* to do. It's a life-long apprenticeship. 'What is art,' said John Masefield, 'but delightful work?'

All the same, occasionally people get stuck, or lose confidence. The delight evaporates. Writers can feel (or *be*) locked down. This book is one way of unlocking mental doors.

The reading texts here precede the writing prompts, because we need to read as poets before we can write as poets. It may be useful, and fun (depending on your circumstances), to talk about the reading sections with friends. The sample poems are chosen for their accessibility and human interest, and because each contains at least one technique of particular interest. The writing suggestions follow. They offer a chance to try things out, or take off into an idea of your own.

We suggest you tackle one section at a time. Give it space and thought before moving to the next. It's a good idea to write down your thoughts about someone else's poem before starting to work on one of your own. All writing is good for you: it's your mental exercise, your warm-up. It makes your brain supple and flexible and word-friendly.

If you don't like one of the sections (or sample poems) *at all*, don't worry. Turn the page. Try another. They can be approached in any order.

Helena Nelson & Sue Butler

TOUCHSTONES

PEACHES

Truly they're God's own fruit, glowing
like little suns. We name their juice *nectar.*
Apples and pears can't rival their tender
beauty. And yet they struggle, don't know
how to handle the market's jostle. They keep
to themselves, try and avoid the mêlée
of bruising fingers. Then a careless nail
nicks the velvety blush, leaves them weeping.

No wonder so many evolve, adapt.
Their view is opaque, tightly curved.
We knock on the tin. Perhaps they're asleep?
They can't be touched. In their dark world
they sit motionless, doped with syrup,
not sure if they're hiding or trapped.

Alan Buckley

Reading

'Peaches' is from Alan Buckley's first collection, *Touched* (2020).

You'll notice the poem presents itself as a sonnet, with a physical division between octet and sestet. In the first eight lines the peaches are in the market. From line nine, they're in the can.

The poem's about peaches, yes. What else does it seem to you to be about? Which individual words are (for you) 'hottest' in terms of emotional punch?

What other sonnet 'rules' are apparent? Does there seem to be a rhyme pattern, for example?

Take a look at the sentence structures. Some enjamb. Others are blunt and brief. One line has two whole sentences inside it. There's considerable variety of sentence types and lengths. Are your own sentence structures as widely varied (take a look at a couple of your own poems)?

What do you think of the line 'Their view is opaque, tightly curved'? Isn't it *peaches* that curve, not their view? And anyway, peaches can't see. What's going on here?

Is there anything you could learn from here—or use?

Notes

[*The Notes pages in this book are for anything you like.*]

Writing

Try writing about what you touch, or what touches you.

Don't worry about the form of the writing. Just let it spill out naturally and without editing or correcting as you go along. Break the lines whenever you feel like it.

Start with the literal experience of touch first thing in the morning. Your duvet when you wake. Your feet sliding into your slippers. The wood of the bannister under your hand as you go downstairs. The weight of the kettle as you fill it with water. The feel of your favourite mug in your fingers.

Then write about what touches you emotionally as you go about your day. Sunlight on your face. Someone laughing (or crying). A tree being chopped down (or planted). The purr of your cat. The cry of a child. A song on the radio.

And/or you might write about some of the things in your home that touch each other. Sheets, plates in the cupboard, books on the shelves, paper in the printer, cookies in the jar.

IN SICKNESS AND IN HEALTH

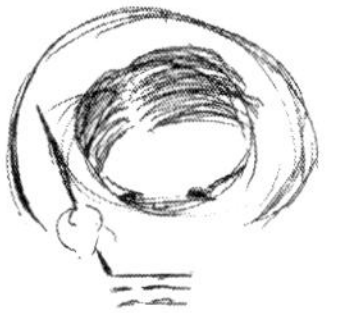

INFLUENZA

The nearest we come again to the pure
passivity of a child is when ill
we lose all initiative and power,
and the animal body wells back up to fill
the vacancy left by a folding self.
The raw and swelling senses, reborn,
freed from will and action, return
to first impressions. Now the sun is felt
warm as gold, immanent in every room,
glorified even in the bathroom chintzes;
a solitary dog barks down the distances
of August fields; downstairs there is a low hum
of voices, the strength toward which we fall,
blissfully, as if towards something eternal.

Tom Duddy

Reading

'Influenza' appeared in Tom Duddy's posthumous collection *The Years* (2014). You'll notice it's a 14-liner, so you might want to consider whether the poet was thinking of it as a sonnet, and if so, what sort of formal patterns it contains.

'Influenza' is a 'we' poem throughout (first person plural). So the experience is generalised to all of us. You don't see many 'we' poems. How well does this work for you?

Can you track down any similes or metaphors? How interesting/effective are they?

Reading aloud, do you notice the way the 'L' sounds ripple right through the poem? What effect do you think this has?

'Pure passivity' is an unusual phrase, made odder by the line break between adjective and noun. What could it mean?

In a sonnet, there's often a change of direction (or a 'volta') at line nine. Here perhaps it comes half-way along line eight?

What do you take the adjective 'immanent' to mean here?

Would you choose to write a poem in the first person plural yourself (a 'we' poem)? And if so, what kind of topic might it suit?

Is there anything you could learn from here—or use?

Notes

Writing

Illness is the doctor to whom we pay most heed; to kindness and knowledge we make promises; only pain we obey.

—Marcel Proust

Without anxiety and illness I should have been like a ship without a rudder.

—Edvard Munch

How high is your threshold for physical pain? Do you fear catching (then maybe spreading) a contagious disease? Is indignity and reliance on others for basic needs what fills you with horror?

Write about the disease, incapacity or illness that scares you most. Be specific about your concerns. Try to capture and express true personal apprehensions, rather than those society might deem appropriate.

As you explore this potentially grim subject, ask yourself if there might, just possibly ... maybe ... perhaps ... be some benefit to the disease or illness you fear most.

Once you've finished, try the poem with 'we' instead of 'I'.

Which do you prefer?

JOIN THE QUEUE

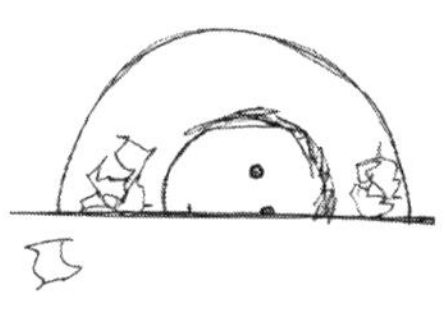

QUEUE

The idea is
you stand here, shuffle along and
when your turn comes she'll
sign your book, and hug you.
Under these arches, though, even
the pigeons are freezing;
the girls ahead and behind me
are both turned, facing others.
The tide's coming in and it's
soaked my plimsolls.
The queue stretches as far as I can
see in both directions.
I'm scared, of course, of losing
my place but the woman
in the distance, signing books
is enunciating
each person's name
carefully, once,
through a tannoy.
I yearn to be closer
but the queue never gets shorter
and the woman stays
small as a worry doll
on the horizon.

Charlotte Gann

Reading

This poem by Charlotte Gann first appeared in *Noir* (2016) and then again (in slightly different form) in the poet's second book, *The Girl Who Cried* (2020). You may have questions of your own after reading it. They might include some of the following.

Where does this queue seem to be? Who might 'the woman' be?

What seems to be the dominant mood (or tone) ?

Supposing the whole poem were a metaphor, what experience might it be representing ?

What do you think the shape contributes? How do the line breaks affect the pacing when you read it aloud?

Most of the words are straightforward. But some are more intense in terms of emotion. Which seem to you most potent?

There's only one simile. What do you think of its positioning?

Is there anything you could learn from here—or use?

Notes

Writing

Join a queue.

There are at least two people in front of you and, very soon, one person behind you; then another two.

Give each person in the queue a voice. Allow them a two-line stanza in which to speak.

However differently they speak, and however diverse the topics, the people in the queue will be connected by the structure: two lines per person; no more, no less.

Leave plenty of white space between each stanza. (As you do this, think about the role white space plays in a poem and how it affects the way your poem might be read.)

KEEPING A RECORD

'HEROES OF OUR ISLANDS'

Dust jacket: faded (sun)
and water stained; torn,
front and back, repairs
(amateur); cracked spine
and wear to corners.
Cover (linen) worn.
Dog-eared, furring on all sides.
Maps partly crayonned in
and marginalia (juvenile).
Some illus., black and white; defaced.

Inscribed: *To dearest John,*
to speed you in their footsteps,
love
from Auntie Joan,
and kisses, Christmas 1959.

D. A. Prince

Reading

The poem first appeared in the author's second collection, *Common Ground* (2014). It's not unlike an entry in a second-hand bookseller's catalogue. No finite verbs, only descriptive participles, and one verb-infinitive in the second stanza ('to speed').

A poem that simply lays down facts (no comments, no story) makes the reader work harder. You infer all sorts of things simply from what is (and isn't) included. It's all 'show' and no 'tell'.

How does 'Heroes of Our Islands' *differ* from the record in a second-hand bookseller's catalogue?

What have you learned about 'dearest John'—or anything else?

Does the poem rhyme?

Whose footsteps?

Is there anything you could learn from here—or use?

Notes

Writing

You're unaware of having committed any crime and yet you're locked in your own home—along with the people who usually live there. You have heat, light and all your things; but the doors won't open, and when you try to climb out of a window, a force-field pushes you back. Once a week, someone leaves groceries on your doorstep. You have no idea how long this will continue.

Before the advent of photography and film, poetry was one way of creating a historical record—think of Tennyson's 'The Charge of the Light Brigade', Wilfred Owen's 'Dulce et Decorum est', etc.

Each day you're imprisoned, use poetry to record one single fact about your situation. Not a generalisation or a cliché but a single specific, detailed fact. Record for posterity things that might otherwise be forgotten.

Place one fact after another. Collect them. See what you've got. This piece of writing may take a while.

TAKING A BREATH

FLY FLYING

A house-fly woozily browses the economy cabin
miles above the Atlantic

and somewhere a mouse is scurrying out of a cargo ship
and nosing deeper into the dock,

a virus is crossing the bridge of a kiss
made urgent after a long separation

and a joke is being told in a new language,
half a world from where it was invented.

The fly twists onto the plane's plastic ceiling,
reeled in by a reading light.

It tiptoes the injection-moulded contours
of an overhead locker, upside down

and somewhere a child is wondering
whether a moth can fly through rain,

and does a birdcage weigh less when the bird is flying,
assuming there is room to fly.

Stephen Payne

Reading

'Fly Flying' is drawn from Stephen Payne's first collection *Pattern Beyond Chance* (2015). Set partly in an aeroplane, it creates airy space between its couplets. If reading it aloud, you'll probably find yourself taking a breath at the end of each stanza. The formal structure takes the reader on a kind of thought-journey in time and space.

Although the individual stanzas are short, the act of connecting them in your mind involves mighty swoops. You go from a fly flying inside an aeroplane (stanza one) to a mouse slinking out of a cargo ship onto shore (stanza two) to a virus passing (somewhere) from one person to another (stanza three) and so on. Small things, big journeys.

The fly on the plane is the only creature that features twice. It inhabits three stanzas in total. Why would that be?

Two stanzas begin 'And somewhere'. Is that accidental or does it have a purpose?

Who is thinking all this? Who is watching that fly? What difference would it make if the poem began in the first person? e.g.
'I watch a house-fly woozily browsing the economy cabin ...'?

You might track the verbs through the poem, and watch their transitions. Just for interest.

Is there anything in this poem you could learn from, or use?

Notes

Writing

A full stop in a poem gives you a place to breathe. Sometimes the end of a line, or a stanza does the same.

But how often are you aware of your breathing?

Today, stop taking breath for granted and start noticing it, especially when reading a poem aloud to yourself.

Be aware of the journey your breath makes as it enters and leaves your lungs. Feel it bringing you the gift of oxygen and removing carbon dioxide.

Notice how different your breath tastes as it enters and leaves your physical body. Be honest about your breath's smell.

Hear your breath; really listen; get to know its music.

What does it feel like to hold that breath?

Now write the longest, or shortest, poem you possibly can, using only six sentences; or only six breaths.

CASUALTY

PÉRI EN MER
(Cameret)

One day the friends who stand about my bed
  Will slowly turn from it to speak of me
Indulgently, as of the newly dead,
  Not knowing how I perished by the sea,
That night in summer when the gulls topped white
  The crowded masts cut black against a sky
Of fading rose—where suddenly the light
  Of Youth went out, and I, no longer I,
Climbed home, the homeless ghost I was to be.
  Yet as I passed, they sped me up the heights—
Old seamen round the door of the Abri
  De la Tempête. Even on quiet nights
  So may some ship go down with all her lights
Beyond the sight of watchers on the quay!

Charlotte Mew (1869 – 1928)

Reading

This very regular sonnet is about an inner death: the point where the poet's spirit guttered. It may remind you of Stevie Smith's 'Not Waving But Drowning' ('Nobody heard him, the dead man / But still he lay moaning'). What an interesting idea—to be both dead *and* alive.

Equally interesting is the fact that the poet has remembered so clearly the precise moment at which everything changed, even though nothing specific (apparently) happened.

What's the setting/situation in the first three lines? It's a future vision—of what?

If you had to paint that 'night in summer', could you *see* it? How visual is the description?

Two rhyming sounds recur noticeably, first appearing in 'me' and 'white'. You may not have noticed rhyme-echoes at the end of 'indulgently' and suddenly'. Or the way 'nights', 'lights' and 'sight' are so close together at the end (lines 12 and 13 are the only two lines with adjoining rhymes, though both 'night' and 'white' appear in line 5). The construction of the poem is carefully planned and intricate.

Does 'Abri de la Tempête' suggest to you that Charlotte Mew is remembering a real place? Or has she chosen it because of the shelter in a storm the name implies? Is it significant that she goes '*up* the heights'? Is the word 'passed' important?

Is there anything in this poem you could learn from, or use?

Notes

Writing

Children show scars like medals. Lovers use them as a secret to reveal. A scar is what happens when the word is made flesh.

—Leonard Cohen, 'The Favourite Game'

Forget a muddy trench in France, or Napoleon's army retreating from Borodino—what are the theatres of war in which *you* have been wounded? (e.g. the playground, your kitchen, your workplace, a courtroom.)

And forget about guns, tanks and surface-to-air missiles—what other things wound? (e.g. sharks, open-cast mines, wills, theft, jealousy, words.)

Pick a situation in which you were injured. Then write about it. You might include the following details:

How severe was your wound? Did anybody notice?

Who was your assailant? Or did you shoot yourself in the foot? What treatment did your wound require?

How effective was the healing power of time, chocolate cake, prayer, friends, pets or a song?

OPEN AND SHUT

POSTCARD

Three days and already I could write
a dissertation on the fastenings of gates:

the counterintuitive, industry standard
grey metal latch, to be clanged backwards;

the bolt with a spring that's always too strong;
the soft warmth of an old chain, brown stream

through fingers, binding the post with a hook;
the double gate's hard-edged central loop

with its guillotine rise/drop; and the frayed
Gordian knot of orange nylon twine, avoided

by climbing at the hinge end. Each one
a puzzle, each to be handled and worked on,

each gate lifted or pulled before I pass
from the last room of sheep or meadow flowers—

below hills that move up and down and up
as if walking their own walk—to the next. With love.

Fiona Moore

Reading

This poem is drawn from the author's first full collection, *The Distal Point* (2018). Do you know the unwritten rule about repetition in poems? Repeat a word twice and it could be a slip. But repeat it three times, and it must be deliberate. There are three 'gate' mentions here, so no accident.

The poem goes through the gates of its stanzas, each opening and closing and leading to the next, some fluidly enjambed; others linked by punctuation. The only stanza that ends with a full stop is the last one.

What do you think the poem is about—apart from gates?

Are there any sound patterns? Rhymes?

How important is the title?

Which word in the poem has most syllables? Do you think it earns its place?

The parenthesis (between 'flowers' and 'to the next') in the last stanza, makes the sentence at first tricky to follow. Is this okay? Is it deliberate?

Is there anything in this poem you could learn from, or use?

Notes

Writing

A poem's title is its gate. The poet's aim is to make the reader want to open the gate and go through—not just once, but time and time again.

Make a list of all the gates you can think of e.g. Watergate, Margate, Bill, five-bar, Hell's, Pearly, level-crossing, leg, prison, portcullis, garden, and so on.

Now try one or more of the following:

* Have a dialogue with a gatekeeper.

* *Segregate, relegate, litigate, delegate.*

* Play with proverbs. A gate in time saves—, a gate in need is—, a watched gate never—

* Leave a gate open, either accidentally or deliberately. What are the consequences?

* Describe a (literal or metaphorical) gate to someone who lives in a world with no gates.

* Eat gateaux outside a street cafe. Make your reader jealous.

GREEN FINGERS

A POISON TREE

I was angry with my friend:
I told my wrath, my wrath did end.
I was angry with my foe:
I told it not, my wrath did grow.

And I water'd it in fears,
Night & morning with my tears;
And I sunnèd it with smiles,
And with soft deceitful wiles.

And it grew both day and night,
Till it bore an apple bright;
And my foe beheld it shine,
And he knew that it was mine,

And into my garden stole,
When the night had veil'd the pole:
In the morning glad I see
My foe outstretch'd beneath the tree.

William Blake (1757 – 1827)

Reading

This unforgettable Blake poem is one of the 'experience' set in his illustrated volume 'Songs of Innocence and Experience'. The first four lines are like a proverb. By the end of line 4 the moral precept is complete. But the poem continues. It goes somewhere you hardly expect.

In a first-person poem, the reader identifies with the narrator, and expects to be the 'good guy'. Here the narrator turns out to be a killer. The murder's carefully planned. There is not one scrap of remorse.

You might notice the deceptive simplicity of the sentence structures. You might consider why Blake chose an apple tree (it could have been any fruit).

You might think about the issue of deceit (there's deception on both sides, friend and foe).

You might think about the effect of the sudden shift into the present tense in the last two lines.

And you might wonder exactly what the poem is saying about human nature.

Finally, is there anything you could learn from this poem—or use in one of your own?

Notes

Writing

Seeds are amazing capsules of energy. Given the right conditions, they grow into something that survives for a few months, or even for centuries. So whether you live in an apartment with a window-box or have a huge garden—go on, get planting.

Yes, you could press a seed into a pot of compost, water it and write about what happens next.

But how about planting some seeds of doubt? What colour are they? What size? What do they need to flourish? How long do doubt seeds take to grow, and can you eat the fruit?

You are a horticultural expert. In the style of a person who knows about plants, explain how to handle doubt seeds for best results.

Or

Write in couplets (like Blake's) and allow rhyme to dictate what might emerge from a packet of seeds, however bizarre.

COME RAIN OR SHINE

RAIN

Rain, midnight rain, nothing but the wild rain
On this bleak hut, and solitude, and me
Remembering again that I shall die
And neither hear the rain nor give it thanks
For washing me cleaner than I have been
Since I was born into solitude.
Blessed are the dead that the rain rains upon:
But here I pray that none whom once I loved
Is dying tonight or lying still awake
Solitary, listening to the rain,
Either in pain or thus in sympathy
Helpless among the living and the dead,
Like a cold water among broken reeds,
Myriads of broken reeds all still and stiff,
Like me who have no love which this wild rain
Has not dissolved except the love of death,
If love it be towards what is perfect and
Cannot, the tempest tells me, disappoint.

Edward Thomas (1887 – 1917)

Reading

This poem was written in January 1916. The First World War was raging. The poet had enlisted in the British Army but had not yet seen active service (he was killed at Arras in April 1917.)

The dominant metre of 'Rain' is iambic pentameter, and most of the lines have ten syllables. But the rhythm of the first line is jagged and uneven. Why might that be?

There are many repetitions. Can you track all words that are either repeated exactly, or similarly? Do you draw any conclusions from doing that?

The last two lines contain words that appear nowhere else. Why might that be? What effect does it have?

How many words here rhyme or half-rhyme with 'rain'?

From the start of line 7 ('Blessed are the dead ...'), the whole of the rest of the poem is a single sentence. Does the poet manage that sentence securely? Do you follow his train of thought right through to the end, without any hitches?

When you shut your eyes after reading the poem, which of its images (if any) can you 'see' clearly?

What do you think Edward Thomas means by these lines:

> 'And neither hear the rain nor give it thanks
> For washing me cleaner than I have been
> Since I was born into solitude.'

Finally, is there anything you could learn from here—or use?

Notes

Writing

Do you only think about the weather when it spoils your plans? Act differently today. Go to the window or step outside and introduce yourself. Then give today's weather a voice. Have a dialogue with him or her.

If it happens to be raining, try writing six 5-line stanzas about about six different types of rain.

Or imagine you have control of the weather for the whole world—not just for today but for the coming twelve months.

What weather will you give yourself and your friends? Will it snow in the Australian outback? Will anyone get a typhoon?

Or can you imagine a year—no, make that *three*—when you wake each morning to exactly the same weather?

How do you feel? How do you behave?

AN ACCUMULATION

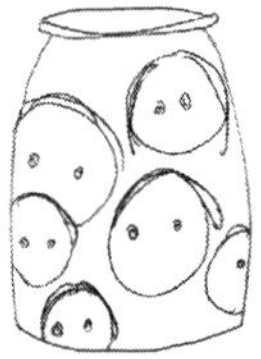

THIS IS THE HOUSE THAT JACK BUILT

This is the house that Jack built.

This is the malt
that lay in the house that Jack built.

This is the rat
That ate the malt
That lay in the house that Jack built.

This is the cat
That killed the rat
That ate the malt
That lay in the house that Jack built.

This is the dog
That worried the cat
That killed the rat
That ate the malt
That lay in the house that Jack built.

This is the cow with the crumpled horn,
That tossed the dog
That worried the cat
That killed the rat
That ate the malt
That lay in the house that Jack built.

This is the maiden all forlorn,
That milked the cow with the crumpled horn,
That tossed the dog,
That worried the cat,
That killed the rat,

That ate the malt
That lay in the house that Jack built.

This is the man all tattered and torn,
That kissed the maiden all forlorn,
That milked the cow with the crumpled horn,
That tossed the dog,
That worried the cat,
That killed the rat,
That ate the malt
That lay in the house that Jack built.

This is the priest all shaven and shorn
That married the man all tattered and torn,
That kissed the maiden all forlorn,
That milked the cow with the crumpled horn,
That tossed the dog,
That worried the cat,
That killed the rat,
That ate the malt
That lay in the house that Jack built.

This is the cock that crowed in the morn,
That waked the priest all shaven and shorn,
That married the man all tattered and torn,
That kissed the maiden all forlorn,
That milked the cow with the crumpled horn,
That tossed the dog,
That worried the cat,
That killed the rat,
That ate the malt
That lay in the house that Jack built.

This is the farmer sowing his corn,
That kept the cock that crowed in the morn,
That woke the priest all shaven and shorn,
That married the man all tattered and torn,
That kissed the maiden all forlorn,
That milked the cow with the crumpled horn,
That tossed the dog,
That worried the cat,
That killed the rat,
That ate the malt
That lay in the house that Jack built.

Anon

Reading

'The House that Jack Built' first appeared in published form in 1755, but it's much older than that. It has a rollicking rhythm when you read it aloud, which you absolutely should.

You might work out what you think the love story is. And whether Jack is important (who *is* Jack, after all?). And why was the priest 'shaven and shorn'? And why 'malt'?

Cherrington Manor in Shropshire is allegedly the house that Jack built, whoever Jack may have been. It's an ancient building, recorded in the Domesday book of 1086. Interestingly, it has an old malthouse behind it, i.e. a place where grain (probably barley) would once have been converted into malt, which in turn was used to brew beer or whisky. Or to make malt vinegar. Or extract of malt, which children used to be cajoled to swallow in syrupy form.

Can you see the pattern of verbs in the 'that' clauses, and the way they drive the rhythm? They grow more and more striking as the action progresses, and they're nearly all monosyllables: *lay / ate / killed / kissed / tossed* etc.

In fact, the poem is entirely monosyllabic up to the point where a two-syllable word creeps in. The two-syllable words do something interesting to the rhythm. Can you feel it?

A twentieth-century poem that draws on this sentence pattern is Elizabeth Bishop's remarkable 'Visits to St Elizabeth's'. You might want to track it down and examine the way she uses (but changes) the 'Jack' principle. Her first line is 'This is the house of Bedlam.'

Notes

Writing

Joe Moran, in *First Write a Sentence*, says 'A cumulative sentence is the prose equivalent of the long tracking shot' (in film). The reader doesn't get lost in a sentence of this kind because everything's driven by the first few words.

Each stanza of 'The House that Jack Built' is a single cumulative sentence. It has a subject ('This') and a simple verb ('is'). The group of 'that' clauses gets longer and longer as the story goes on, but all relate to 'This is the house that Jack built'.

It's an easy technique to copy. Your opening statement has to be simple. Perhaps something like this:

> I am the one who gets you up,
> who puts out the breakfast,
> who kisses your nose,
> who straightens your tie,
> who checks you have money,
> who gives you your lunchbox,
> who sends you to school.

or

> I was going to the market
> with my friend Fluff who works in Morrisons
> and my friend Jaki who works in Aldi
> and my friend Daljit who works in Top Trees
> and my friend Ayesha who sells jewellery on Etsy
> and my friend Kat who has no job at all.

Why don't you try a poem in a series of cumulative sentences? You could adopt the precise pattern of 'The House that

Jack Built' but substitute different nouns and verbs (just for fun, and to see what happens). Or you might be a little more adventurous. But no matter how you manage your cumulative sentences, do

* break each line at the end of a clause
* break each stanza at the end of a sentence
* write mainly in monosyllables

Possible topics (or come up with your own):

* making a meal for someone special
* The house that Jill built
* looking for something you've lost
* why the maiden was forlorn
* writing a letter of complaint

Or, of course, you might write Jack's version of events. Or Jill's....